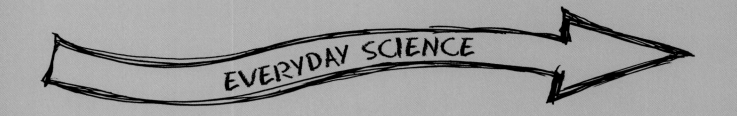

Plants

To my granddaughter, Megan Kate

MH VS

Please visit our web site at: www.garethstevens.com
For a free color catalog describing Gareth Stevens Publishing's list of
high-quality books and multimedia programs, call 1-800-542-2595 (USA)
or 1-800-387-3178 (Canada). Gareth Stevens Publishing's fax: (414) 332-3567.

Library of Congress Cataloging-in-Publication Data

Riley, Peter D.
    Plants / by Peter Riley. — North American ed.
        p. cm. — (Everyday science)
    Summary: A simple introduction to various kinds of plants and the basic concepts
    related to growing plants.
    Includes bibliographical references and index.
    ISBN 0-8368-3718-5 (lib. bdg.)
    1. Plants—Juvenile literature. [1. Plants.] I. Title.
QK49.R543   2003
580—dc21   2003042734

This North American edition first published in 2004 by
Gareth Stevens Publishing
A World Almanac Education Group Company
330 West Olive Street, Suite 100
Milwaukee, Wisconsin 53212 USA

Original text © 2003 by Peter Riley. Images © 2003 by Franklin Watts.
First published in 2003 by Franklin Watts, 96 Leonard Street, London, EC2A 4XD, England.
This U.S. edition copyright © 2004 by Gareth Stevens, Inc.

Series Editor: Sarah Peutrill
Designer: Ian Thompson
Photography: Ray Moller (unless otherwise credited)
Photo Researcher: Diana Morris
Gareth Stevens Editor: Carol Ryback
Gareth Stevens Designer: Melissa Valuch

Picture Credits: (t) top, (b) bottom, (c) center, (l) left, (r) right
A–Z Botanical Collection: /G. W. Miller, p. 16(tl). Bruce Coleman Collection: /Dr. Eckhart Pott, p. 9(b); /Iain Sarjeant, p. 14(cr).
Ecoscene: /Graham Kitching, p. 14(cl). Chris Fairclough, p. 16(b). FLPA: /M. Nimmo, p. 13(b). Papilio: /Robert Pickett, p. 10(b).
Photogenes: /Diana Morris, p. 7. Gregg Andersen, p.17.

The original publisher thanks the following children for modeling for this book: Amber Barkhouse, Reece Calvert, Shani-e Cox,
Chantelle Daniel, Ammar Duffus, Alex Green, Harry Johal, and Emily Scott.

Printed in Hong Kong

1 2 3 4 5 6 7 8 9 07 06 05 04 03

Plants

Written by Peter Riley

Gareth Stevens Publishing
A WORLD ALMANAC EDUCATION GROUP COMPANY

About This Book

Everyday Science is designed to encourage children to think about their everyday world in a scientific way, by examining cause and effect through close observation and discussing what they have seen. Here are some tips to help you get the most from **Plants**.

- This book introduces the basic concepts of plant life and some of the vocabulary associated with them, such as flowers, leaves, stems, and roots, and it prepares children for more advanced learning about plants.

- You can extend the work on page 7 by having the children look at a collection of houseplants. Ask the children to group the plants according to whether the plants have flowers and by the colors of their flowers.

- You can extend the work on page 9 by drying some pinecones until they open. After the cones are dried, ask the children to shake the cones so that the seeds fall out.

- On pages 19 and 23, children are invited to predict the results of a particular action or test. Discuss the reason for any answer they give in some depth before turning the page. For the question on page 19, look for an answer about how the seeds will not grow without water because plants need water to grow. The process of a seed sprouting and growing into a plant is called germination. Seeds must have water in order to germinate. For the question on page 23, look for an answer about plants needing light to stay healthy. Plants use light to make food in their leaves.

Contents

Kinds 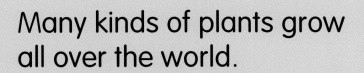 of Plants

Many kinds of plants grow all over the world.

A fern plant has leaves with ragged edges that look like feathers.

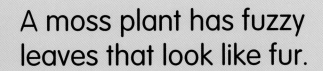

A moss plant has fuzzy leaves that look like fur.

Many plants grow flowers that have bright colors.

Trees and bushes are plants that are woody.

Point to the trees, bushes, and flowers
in this picture.

Parts of a Plant

Each part of a plant has a name. Some of the parts of a plant are its flowers, leaves, stem, and roots.

flowers

leaves

stem

roots

Not all plants have flowers.

Ferns can grow brown patches under their leaves instead of flowers.

Pine trees grow pinecones instead of flowers.

Roots

Roots grow underground.

Roots soak up water from the soil.

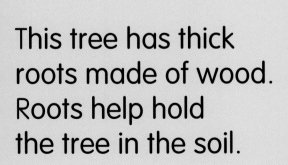

This tree has thick roots made of wood. Roots help hold the tree in the soil.

This plant has been growing in its pot for a long time.

The roots have grown for so long that they circle around the bottom of the pot.

The plant must be moved to a larger pot. This is called repotting.

Stems

The stem holds up the leaves and flowers of a plant. Some plants have only one stem.

Some plants have many stems.

Some plants have stems that are hidden by leaves.

A tree has a woody stem called a trunk.
The trunk is covered with bark.

Every year, the tree grows a new ring of wood
inside its trunk. The trunk becomes wider as
the tree gets older.

Count the rings
of this tree. Is
this tree older
or younger
than you?

Leaves

Leaves have different shapes, colors, and sizes.

Some trees lose their leaves in autumn. They grow new leaves in spring.

Some trees keep their leaves all year. They stay green all year and are called evergreens.

Flowers

Some plants grow many little flowers.

Some plants grow one large flower.

The colored parts of a flower are called the petals. How many petals does this flower have?

What forms inside a flower? Turn the page to find out.

Seeds

Seeds form inside a flower. Seeds can grow into more plants with flowers.

Sometimes seeds grow inside a fruit.

Sometimes seeds grow inside pods.

Seeds from different plants do not all look the same. Seeds of different plants may be different sizes, shapes, and colors.

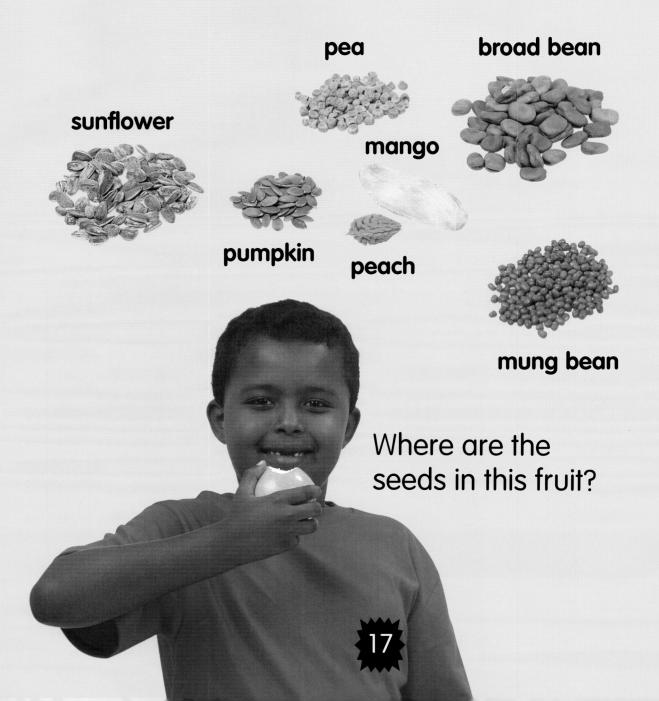

pea

broad bean

sunflower

mango

pumpkin

peach

mung bean

Where are the seeds in this fruit?

Planting Seeds

Laura and Sam are planting seeds.

They put
soil into pots.

They make
four holes in
the soil.

They put a
pea seed in
each hole.

They cover the
seeds with soil.

Sam waters
his seeds.

Laura does not
water her seeds.

What do you think will happen after a few days?
Turn the page to find out.

Seedlings

Sam's seeds have grown stems and roots. The tiny plants are called seedlings.

When seeds grow stems and roots, we say they germinate.

Laura's seeds have not grown stems or roots. Why do you think they have not germinated?

This plant has not been watered. Its leaves are droopy and look wilted.

Nicole waters the plant so that it will soak up water.

After a few hours, the plant stops wilting.

Too Much Water

Too much water harms plants.

If the soil in the pot feels wet, do not water the plant.

If the soil in the pot feels dry, give the plant a small amount of water.

Feel the soil of your houseplants at home before watering them. Ask an adult to help you.

Nicole and Matthew have alfalfa seedlings.

Nicole puts her seedlings in a place with plenty of light.

Matthew puts his seedlings in a dark place.

What do you think will happen to the seedlings in a few days? Turn the page to find out.

Light Tests

Nicole's seedlings grew into plants with dark green leaves and short, firm stems.

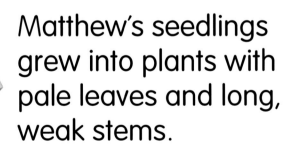

Matthew's seedlings grew into plants with pale leaves and long, weak stems.

Try this test with some other kinds of seeds.

Sam sets up a test to see if plants grow toward the light. He makes a cover with a hole cut in one side.

Here is the hole.

Sam leaves the cover over the plants for a few days.

After a few days, the plants look like this.

What does Sam's test show?

Plants We Eat

Most of our food comes from plants.

We eat the flowers and stems of the broccoli plant.

We eat the leaves of the lettuce plant.

We eat the fruit of orange trees.

We eat the roots of carrot plants.

Peas are the seeds of the pea plant.

Bread is made from the seeds of the wheat plant.

What part of these plants do you eat? Make a table like the one below to mark your answers.

	root	leaf	stem	flower	seed	fruit
potato	✓					
apple tree						
tomato plant						
sunflower						
cabbage						

Useful Words

bark: the outside layer that covers a tree.

flowers: the parts of plants that make the seeds. Flowers are often brightly colored.

fruits: the parts of some plants that can be eaten and that hold the seeds.

germinate: to start to grow a stem and roots.

houseplants: plants that are grown in pots and kept indoors.

leaves: the flat, usually green, parts of a plant that can grow from the main stem or from a branch off the main stem.

roots: the parts of a plant that go down into the soil to soak up water and hold the plant firmly in the ground.

seeds: the usually tiny parts made by a plant that can grow into new plants.

seedlings: young plants that have just started to grow from seeds.

stem: the main part of the plant. The stem is usually long and thin.

trunk: the woody stem of a tree.

Some Answers

Here are some answers to the questions asked in this book. If you had different answers, you may be right, too. Talk over your answers with other people and see if you can explain why they are right.

page 13   The tree trunk has more than thirty rings, which means the tree is more than thirty years old.

page 15   The flower has six petals.

page 17   The dark seeds of an apple are found near the core, or the center, of the fruit.

page 20   Laura's seeds have not germinated because they did not have any water. Seeds need water and warmth to germinate.

page 25   Sam's test shows that plants grow toward the light. If you put a potted plant, such as a geranium, on a sunny windowsill, its stems and leaves will grow toward the window.

page 27   We eat the root of a potato plant.

We eat the fruit of an apple tree.

We eat the fruit of a tomato plant (although it is sometimes called a vegetable). Only the fruit of the tomato plant is edible. Other parts of the plant are poisonous.

We eat the seeds of sunflowers.

We eat the leaves of a head of cabbage.

For More Information

More Books to Read

- *How Plants Grow. Plants* (series)
  Angela Royston
  (Heinemann Library)

- *The Reason for a Flower. World of Nature* (series)
  Ruth Heller
  (Paper Star/Penguin Putnam)

- *The Science of Plants. Living Science* (series)
  Jonathan Bocknek
  (Gareth Stevens)

Web Sites

- Biodome
  pbskids.org/zoom/sci/biodome.html

- Michigan 4H Children's Garden
  4hgarden.msu.edu/main.html

Index